Praise for R

"Rebel Song is not a call to arms, it is a call to awareness and conscience, a plea for consideration of the plight of ourselves and our fellow men and women—for our civilization. Unlike any other such plea, it is marvelously poetic, filled with imagery, metaphors, alliteration, rhyme—a genuine poetic masterpiece that strikes at all of our hearts and opens them to the need for action. It will be remembered for years as a defining statement of the soul of today's disenfranchised everyman, crying out for justice."
- Casey Dorman, Author, Editor: Lost Coast Review

"In Rebel Song, *Rivera Sun* writes in the tradition of Whitman, Jeffers and June Jordan, poems that testify to the indomitable spirit that is alive in the resistance. This work is gritty and visceral and of the earth. To me it felt like that clarion call I have been waiting for which combines poetry and activism . . . Profound and hopeful, this book is a touchstone for remembering how crucial our voices are for the evolution of the spirit and the survival of the soul."- Devreaux Baker, Poet, Pen Oakland Award winner for her book, *Red Willow People.*

"This grand poem reminds us that the rebel, the body of rebellion, is made up of many ordinary women/men, and the storm, of love in action. The decline of Mother Earth and her children is only inevitable if we, the ordinary, fail to rise. Its metaphors are extended, visual, and engaging. I thought the epic poem was a lost art. It seems to have been found in the rising winds of a love-storm."
– Rob Ganson, Poet, *Follow the River Clear Down*

"Rebel Song is a powerful poem that stands not only as an anthem for our global peace and justice movement, but also takes a much deeper step to examine the heart from which we operate, to touch the tears that teach - and the fierce love that inspires - where they live inside us."
- Diane Patterson, Singer/Songwriter, Folkgoddess

"This is poignant, powerful, beautiful, heart-wrenching, heart-warming and so much more. A clear stand for justice (as in all Rivera Sun's work) that opens a door for others to stand up, walk through, AND join the movement."
– Cindy Reinhardt, Writer

Rebel Song

by

Rivera Sun

Rebel Song
Copyright © 2018 by Rivera Sun

All rights reserved. Printed in the United States of America.
No part of this book may be used or reproduced in any
manner whatsoever without written permission except in the
case of brief quotations embodied in critical articles and
reviews. For information address:

Rising Sun Press Works
P.O. Box 1751, El Prado, NM 87529
www.riverasun.com

Library of Congress Control Number
2015947466

ISBN
Paperback: 978-0-9966391-0-1
Ebook: 978-0-9966391-1-8

Sun, Rivera 1982-
Rebel Song

This is a work of fiction. Names, characters, places, and
incidents either are the product of the author's imagination or
are used fictitiously. Any resemblance to actual persons, living
or dead, events, companies, or locales is entirely coincidental.
Cover illustration by Rivera Sun

Dedicated to the Rebels

Table of Contents

*Note: Rebel Song is a powerful poem–story
that comes alive when read aloud. An audio
version of Rivera Sun reading Rebel Song
is available on Audible and in other
audiobook formats.*

Part One:
The Storm

Shhh. Listen . . .
Hear it?
On the road?
Far off
but coming
closer.

Change.

Like a black cloud
a dust storm
a locust swarm
or an army on the march.

These are the times when I wonder.

These are the nights
when my certainty quivers
like an old house quaking in the wind.
The floorboards groan,
foundation shudders,
my mind shivers
as icy drafts
of chilling thoughts
sweep across,
rob my warmth,
steal my calm
then vanish.
Leaving me
nothing,
a nobody
all alone,
on my own,
just a woman like any other,
common, ordinary
except . . .
awake!

While the country snores,
smacks its lips,
sighs in sleep,
or stumbles home
in drunken stupors,
banged up, black-eyed
from the bars,
I sit silent,
on alert,
wide awake
and
frozen stiff as stars
that crack the ice-black sky.

These are the nights when I wonder.

My heart is pacing, skittish,
like an old dog, hearing
danger in the dark,
threats on the road,
staring at the door with

a growl on her lips,
hackles on her back
rising.

Lay down, dog!
Stay calm, heart!
You're making me nervous.
Nothing's out there.

Courage is a matchstick
snapped up against the dark.
Worry is the draft
that blows it out.

Stay calm, my heart, lie still.
Nothing's going to happen tonight.

Look, there's a party
at the Big House,
where the wealthy all have gathered.
The lights are on across the way

as the band does battle
with the wind.

A long line of cars
turns up the drive.
Headlight eyes
cold motored gazes
like deer frozen,
locked in disaster.

Shhh. Listen.
Hear that?

A cry of laughter
broke the night,
high-pitched, hanging
at hysteria's edge.
That laughter knows . . .
the woman knows . . .
perhaps, the Big House knows . . .
there is something coming

on the road for us tonight.
And this may be the last party
for us all.

Even if I had been invited,
I shouldn't, couldn't, wouldn't go,
but even so,
I laid out my dress
a white thing, thin,
like a shroud,
like a sacrificial virgin,
or a peeled-off layer of my skin.
A too-thin thing
to wear on such a night.

When that laughter knows . . .
the dog-heart knows . . .
the Big House ought to know,
there is something
coming on the road
for us tonight.

And the lights across the way
blaze bright in denial.
The band plays on, oblivious.
They raise their toasts, regardless.
Flirt and bicker, crack their jokes,
snap out petty arguments,
gossip in malicious whispers,
smile falsely to each other . . .

. . . as if a storm of change
were not blowing down the road.

This is not a night
for skin-thin dresses
or sacrificial shrouds.
It is a night to hunker down
and anchor to the rocks,
pray to whatever saints are listening
to help us all survive
what is coming
down the road.

For I can hear it rumbling,
the ground - the rock - is shaking,
the earth beneath me, shuddering,
and I am but a frail-flesh child
clinging to my mother.

This mother earth that I hold tight
may slip my grip tonight.

What is coming in that storm?
A reckoning?
A settling of debts?
Retribution for injustices
left smoldering too long?

My heart is scratching at the door,
wanting to find out.

Fine then, go!
Go, my heart,
my faithful dog.

Go sniff out truth
and tell me.
But hurry back!
Be careful, heart!
Don't get caught.
Don't get shot.
Don't be seen.
Don't be trapped.
Go sniff out truth
and hurry back!

This house is cold
without you.
The drafty thoughts
bite to the bone.
I am alone
at home
with the lonesome
wind's moan
the only sound around.

These are the nights
when I wonder.

When my mind travels down
the darkened path
of roads less traveled,
and questions left unasked.
These are the nights
when I wonder . . .
about the world beyond my door,
about the never-ending parties,
about mansions built
on backs of men,
about women's tears
that wash the floors,
about old people's fears
that wax them,
about the blood
that's hung in the red velour,
about thick curtains of denial,
about patterned violence

papering walls,
about glass windows stained
with constant lies,
and poisoned rivers
sacrificed for fountains.

These are the nights
when I wonder . . .
how long the band will play
and who are the trumpeters
with cheeks bright red
puffing profit piper tunes?
Who are the violinists
striking rich men's chords,
strumming strings of luxury,
drowning cries of suffering?

For shame on those who play so loud
that those partiers cannot hear
wailing children in the night,
screaming women,

sobbing men!
For shame on those
who would cook a feast
while people scrounge in dumpsters!

For shame, I suppose,
but how can I lay blame
when I could have been like them?
I look across at the Big House
blazing against the night
and I know them.
Servants, served, and masters, all,
I could have been like them.
So who am I to blame?
Hunger knocks on all men's doors.
Evictions arrive with the morning news
brought by whistling delivery boys
riding carelessly,
spared eviction's fate
by handing it to others.

Who can blame the line of cars
parked along the drive?
The eager social climbers
clamoring to the party?
Rats on a sinking, dying ship,
scrambling for safety.

Who can blame the women
- the wives of other men -
who slip between
the silken sheets
in the bedroom of the host?

The bed is warm.
The night is long.
The future dark and cold.
Hunger knocks on every door.

Who can blame the sell-out souls
playing poker with the devil?

Every man toasts to his own success
and drowns his conscience in oblivion.

So, why bother blaming them,
for what I, myself, might do?

To stay sober is a road
through heartbreak.
To stay honest is a lonely path.
Even I who have walked
this road for years,
might have strayed from it tonight.

See? I laid out my dress,
skin-thin, bone-white,
and placed my party shoes beneath it.
I had no pearls to string my neck.
My lipstick is but a stub.
But I would have put them on tonight
and walked across the way,
except my heart

- my faithful heart! -
would not let me go.

My heart would not let me
put on that dress,
nor paint my lips bright red.
My heart forced me
to stay home tonight
and listen to the wind.

Such a beautiful dress.
A shame,
a shame to wear it,
a shame to not.
Such a shame.
A bone-white
moon bright
gown to be worn
on your wedding night,
skin-tight
just right,

a dress to be buried in.
And tonight
the last night
I might ever get to wear it.

Let's put it on!
Just for a moment,
just for a second,
while the dog-gone heart
can't stop me.

Forget the party across the way.
I'll dance here
in my room
to the wind's tune.
I'll dance to the sound
of what's coming -
the mystery,
uncertainty,
of what will be.

I'll put on this dress of skin
and dance to the change
that is coming.

I'll dance to the storm that will slip
across the Big House floor
flipping tailcoats
lifting skirts
sending servants scurrying,
shutting doors and windows.
Futile! Too little, too late.
This storm's so great,
it will sweep up partiers like paper dolls,
send dry-husk souls a-swirling.
Whole lives will go tumbling
down the road
to who-knows-where
and I know-not-what.
That is the change that is coming.

Shhh! Listen!

Something's at the door!
Not the dog -
she would bark.
It was not the heart that knocked.

"Who is it?" I call,
peering through the crack.

Soldiers!
Running before the storm!
Using the roiling rumble
of change on the horizon
to come pounding at the door.

"Everyone's all over at the party!" I cry.

"What? What's that?
You don't want them?
Not their kind?
It's dissidents, dissenters,
rebels, radicals,

revolutionaries
they're rounding up?!

"What!
You can't -
I'm not -
you're wrong -
there's some mistake -
you can't take me!"

Block the door!
Move the chair!
Push the cabinet across!
They're pounding!
The door's giving!
The window!

Out!

Out into the night! Run!
Run in a gown bone-white!

Fool! Bright against the night!
Fool! A dress skin-tight!
Fool! The soldiers will catch you!

Fool.

Part Two:
Death March

Head. Forward. March.
Look at all these people.
A whole nation's been rounded up
from the rocky mountains,
golden coasts,
towering forests,
scorching deserts,
fertile valleys,
open plains,
crowded cities . . .
but these are not just radicals,
rebels, and revolutionaries.
Dissidence was just an excuse
to come pounding on the doors,
sweeping up ordinary citizens
who were simply trying to survive.

Poor people
counting out their pennies,
scrounging to pay rent,
searching for a recipe
to make something
out of nothing,
rounded up like cattle
while the neighbors watched TV,
mouths gaping open,
minds numb watching,
not the misery unfolding,
but the gladiators on the screen.

Have you seen these gladiators?
Everybody has.
I'm sure you've seen them
in suits and ties
fighting for political power,
feinting, dodging,
putting on a show.

Phhtt, spit on them.
They aren't the champions of me!
Nor of these people rounded up -
mothers, children,
workers, students -
nor of anyone I know.
I couldn't tell you
what they're fighting for.
They don't wear their sponsors' logos.
But, the show is entertaining.
At least, it keeps us
jeering, shouting,
cheering in the stands,
placing our penny bets,
our ridiculous one-cent gambles,
while fortunes are made
behind the scenes
in private meetings and secret deals
that we, the people,
stand no chance of winning.

We aren't the players in this game.
We're the chips upon the table.

Our lives are stacked,
our children,
our air,
our water,
our food, houses, labor, health,
country, communities, earth.
My body,
my heart,
my soul,
are poker chips to them.

They stack me up with all the others.
Throw the dice already rigged.
They may lose today.
They'll win tomorrow.
But you and I
will live and die
as poker chips upon their table.

Faceless, meaningless,
commodities,
abstractions,
resources,
statistics,
capital,
collateral,
that's all we are to them.

See that child up ahead?
Marching beside his mother?
So young he's just learned to walk,
barely out of cradle?
He's marching to his death.

For that is what we're on,
a death march,
a paupers' march,
rounded up by gamblers' greed,
swept up by rich men's orders.

See that father, over there?
His dead child in his arms?
He cannot stop to bury her
and can't bear to leave the body.

Vultures.

You see that woman, there?
They say she killed her children,
so they wouldn't have to suffer
through the agonies of life.

We are marching on a death march
because we are the poorest of the poor.
When people sold their souls
for the immunity of profit,
their wide eyes rolled
toward the ghettos,
the barrios,
the rural hills,
the rundown houses,

the line drawn across statistics,
raised and lowered
in political limbo games
in which officials taunt,
"How low can you go,
before you collapse?
How little money can you live on?
Where can we set
the poverty line,
the hoop you have to jump through,
to get some help,
some food,
some shelter?

"Hah!" an official laughs
as a woman leaps and misses.
He doesn't help her up.

"Hah! Give it a whirl,"
he taunts the next man.
"Dare to jump this, fella?

"Hah! You can't make it,
not with that ball-and-chain,
the iron weight of past convictions.
Get outta here!
You shoulda stopped to think . . .
before you were born
down and out
dirt poor!

"What's that grandma?
You're hungry?
Can't afford the rent?
You see this ear?
It's a special kind of hearing aid,
makes all your whining disappear.
You can buy these now
for a million bucks.
They're for sale
in the rich men's clubs.
But I got mine
as a gift, let's say,

for burning a pile of statistics
things that shoulda
gone on file
a whole stack
of boring stuff,
human rights violations,
corruption, bribery,
frauds, thefts,
and scandals.

"Who cares?
That's life, right?
No sense in worrying
about it now.
I got an eye that's blind
and a hearing aid ear,
and I just turn my head,
so I can't see the poor people
who can't jump the line -
I just see the rich folks' splendor
over there."

Those that could
crossed all lines
to escape being in line with us.
I can see them now
as we pass through towns,
looking out through shuttered windows,
standing cross-armed on the porches,
sneering as we pass,
eyes narrowed in disgust
and fear and knowing
they will be next,
if they don't jeer loud enough at us . . .
if they don't obey their orders . . .
if they don't play the rich man's tune.

But who am I to blame them?
I should not
- cannot -
blame them.

Not I.

Not I, who when this child falls,
will not stop to pick her up
for she is not my child.

My heart is gone,
and just as well,
for now it cannot break.
I am a vacant mind
inside a body . . .
but for those who sit
in what were once our homes,
cozy in what were once our beds,
this body is now a hollow flute
that the winds of change
are playing.

"Listen. Listen,"
my flute-body moans,
"hear the storm that is coming.
It will sweep across the Big House
tossing partiers up like leaves.

You are dust upon these winds.
Today, the soldiers pass your doorstep,
but tomorrow,
look around!
When we are gone
our tracks remain,
a line drawn closer
to your family.
Look around!
Your child is next in line
to be the one that cries
from hunger.
Look around!
Your wife will wear
the broken shoes.
Your hands will clench in pain.
Look around!
My passing feet
are drawing lines
closer to your doorstep."

My words whistle in an empty wind,
falling on deaf ears.

I feel internal fire
start to rise,
my rage and fury,
as we pass by
houses full of stuffed-pork sausages,
people squinty-eyed as pigs,
drawing shutters closed
over human suffering,
refusing to speak out.

Cowards!
This country reeks of piss and fear,
a whole nation of red-eyed rabbits.
I long to lunge at them!
To chase them!
To worry them!
To snap them to their idle feet!

Wait!
What's this I feel
inside my chest?
Not despair
Not numbness . . .
Heart!

Part Three:
Heart's Return

Heart? Heart?
Is that you?
My dog-gone heart?
You're back!

"Shhh," the heart says.
"Keep marching, forward, move.
Your anger was the flame
that lit my way to you.
Now put it out.
It's hot.
You don't need that rage
when you've got heart.

"Now quiet, keep marching, move.

"Don't let on that courage
sits within your chest.
Don't let on that love is back,
and if that woman stumbles,
you will help her up,
and if that child falters,
you will carry her until you drop.
Don't let on that something
more dangerous than guns
has found you once again.

"A heart is a treasure
pinned to the undergarments
of your ribs.
A heart is a tool
hidden beneath your skin.
But a heart can be stolen,
broken,
lost, forgotten,
changed, ignored,
and beaten.

So for now, don't let on
that your heart is back.

Forward, march, and listen.

"I have been," the heart says,
"to the middle of the storm.
I have been to the change
that is coming.
I have crawled on my belly
through the wind whipping bushes.
I have raced through the plains
as the lightning bolted down.
I have treaded through the quagmire
of the flooded-out marshes,
plunged through the rushing,
raging rivers.
I have been to the eye of the storm
that is coming
and these are the forces
that thrust it forward . . .

"When the rich men horde the money,
the storm is coming.
When the land is raped for profit,
the storm is coming.
When programs for the public good
are plundered,
the storm is coming.
When wars break loose
from lying tongues,
the storm is coming.
When poverty starts rising,
the storm is coming.
When life expectancy starts falling,
the storm is coming.
When corporations rule
instead of humans,
the storm is coming.
When lawmakers cease
to listen to people,
the storm is coming, the storm.

"When the earth is thrown off cycle,
the seasons twisted out of turn,
the sky heated,
the ice melted,
the forests razed,
the seas warmed,
the storm is coming,
the storm!

"When families sleep in cardboard boxes
near streets of empty houses,
when half the people make less together
than a single wealthy man,
when the powerful live beyond the law,
and spies snitch on all the others,
the storm is coming,
the storm is coming,
and this is what it says:

"I am the storm, the reckoner.
I am justice truly blind.

I am Compassion's eye awakened.
I am the balancer of the world.
I empty out the overfull,
the small shall grow,
the large decrease,
the light grow dark,
the dark turn bright.
I bring balance to this world.
I am the storm, the reckoner,
but no pawn of God am I.
I'm not here to meter out
His punishments
nor to carry you to heaven.
I did not come to prove you right
or smite your enemies down.
I am change and nothing else,
a child of your choices,
set in motion by your actions,
born from what is past,
shaking up the present,
sweeping clear the future.

If you hear within my howl,
the cries of children,
the screams of women,
the curses of angry men,
it is because they have been
too long ignored,
and through me
they will be heard.
Dying breaths
have made my winds,
dying breaths,
and lovers' vows,
children's wishes,
and old men's dreams,
hopes forgotten,
prayers ignored,
all of that and more.
I am a hailstorm of injustice,
or a shower of blessings falling,
that which lacks, I fill,
that which is horded, I share.

I am the storm, the reckoner.
I am justice truly blind.
I am Compassion's eye awakened.
I am change, and nothing more!"

The dog-heart moans,
and whispers,
"I sat in that storm,
in the eye of that storm,
and watched the maelstrom
swirl around me.
Cities fell before that storm.
Nations shifted places.
Rulers toppled from their thrones.
People rose to power.
Rich men's vaults swept into the sky.
Money fell like rain.
The excess was trimmed.
The thin were fleshed.
The weak were given strength.
The powerful were humbled,

and taught to live as one
among the many.
This is the storm, the reckoner.
This is the change that's coming.
This is the truth I found
when you sent me out,
your dog-heart sniffing at the storm!"

The dog falls silent.
A soldier barks,
"Forward. March. Keep moving!"

And I shudder, shiver, stumble
as I'm walking in the line.

"Where are we going?" the heart
whispers.

I tell her,
we are marching on a death march
because we are the poorest of the poor.

The line was drawn across the sand
and war waged harsh against us.
I saw the shock and scramble,
people scurrying like rats,
frantic to cross to safety's side,
and align themselves with fortune.
For, when the dogs of war
were unleashed on the poor,
those that could
crossed all lines
and left us
as bombs were dropped onto our lives.
No work. Boom!
No assistance. Boom!
No options. Boom!
No hope.

Despair is the silence
of a bombed-out city
where the survivors are left to die.

Those that could
crossed the line
spat on their shoes
to make them shine,
borrowed from the bank,
sent their children to private schools,
so the shell-shocked grime
of the refugee poor
could not rub off
on their offspring.
They crawled into the houses
left vacant by our evictions.
They took the jobs
we could not live on,
and broke the picket lines.
They lauded themselves
for being ruthless,
for getting ahead,
being willing to do the dirty work,
able to crunch the numbers,
that wadded up people's lives

and threw them
in the garbage.

And when the millions of the poor
became nothing more
than trash littering
life's highways,
they sent soldiers out
like trash collectors,
garbage men with guns,
to pick us up at rifle point
and throw us in the landfill.

From the north, the south,
the east, the west . . .
long lines of marchers converge,
citizens of every shade of poor,
no corner of the nation
left unscathed.
No stone of hope
unturned.

"Look," my dog-heart
suddenly hisses,
trembling in my chest.

Up ahead,
in a cloud of dust,
bulldozers growl in the distance,
digging out a grave,
warning lights flashing,
motors roaring,
back-up horns blaring.
The beep-beep-beep
sounding like a heart monitor
that's failing.
Smell of death hits.
Fear-sweat breaks
through the people
all around me.
The long line of dusty heads
stretches ahead
to the pit's edge

then vanishes
beneath the sharp retort
of gunshots.

A ripple passes through the crowd -
the cattle at the slaughterhouse
whites of eyes,
muscles tensed,
the strongest set to bolt!

Where, fools? Where?
Hemmed by guards and certain death,
we take another step.

"They're going to kill us!"
the cry slips out.
Shhh, the mothers hiss.
The children! Don't panic -

Too late, fools!
The children know.

They always know.
They smell the rotting bodies.
They feel the tremors in our arms.
The children know.
They always know.
No sense in lying to them now.

"Hssssst," says a voice. "Over here!"

Part Four:
Madman Road

There is a man
on the side of the road,
a madman,
a wild man,
a man with burning ember eyes.
The soldiers skirt around him,
ignore him,
avoid him if they can.
He runs like wind, they whisper.
He's quick, clever as coyote.
They say he dodges bullets.
The soldiers couldn't catch him
if they tried.

"Hssssst!" he says. "Listen.
Listen to the madman
on the side of the road.

Death is certain.
Life is fleeting.
You are many.
They are few.
Some will fall.
Some will live.
But you all will
die ahead.
Listen to me!
You must break this line
and run!"

"Shut up!" hisses an old woman.
"Shut up, you crazy fool.
God will save us,
not your words.
Look at me, I am old.
These bony legs can't run.
You want my son?
You'll take him.
My daughter cannot run.

Not round like the moon
with the new one coming.
This way may lead to certain death,
but there are a few more steps of life!
Not much time,
but enough,
to tell them how I love them,
that God will save them,
if He's willing,
or if not,
we'll meet again,
in His kingdom, up in heaven.
All of us will meet there -"

"All except the damned,"
the madman answers sharply.
"Your heaven's not for them.
An old woman's fairytale
won't soothe them.
Will it?"

He turns to me
with that sharp-eyed stare.

"You, woman?
How about you?
You have legs.
You can run.
No children strap you down.
I see in your eyes,
you aren't headed to
Father's Kingdom.
Down this road is death,
oblivion,
and nothing else."

"I know you," I say.

"I'm sure you do," he says.

"You're that man
they call the Rebel."

"Not exactly," he shrugs,
"but close enough,
for, in truth,
the Rebel's made
of many ordinary men."

"Don't lie," I snap bitterly.
"If you were ordinary,
you'd be walking in this line."

"I could, you know," he answers.
"I could walk along beside you."

"Ah, but you can run," I argue.

"So can you," he insists.

"I tried that," I admit.
"I failed."

"Well, try again, you fool!

You didn't learn to walk
by stopping when you fell!"

This man, this rebel,
is a respected and reviled man,
detested by some
for the same reasons
others revere him:
He speaks the truth.

The dangerous, heartbreaking,
uncomfortable truth.
The "it's not okay,
it's not going to be okay,
it won't ever be okay,
if we keep going in this way,"
truth.
The kind of truth
that no one likes to hear,
even if you agree.

But maybe we should have listened,
still should listen,
to this man's truth.
For all of this is metaphor,
shadow play,
a dream world,
a theater.
But death is real.
Extinction looms.

That coming storm is growing.

And this forced march
toward extinction,
this trail of tears
that no one likes to talk about,
is real.

As we get up in the morning
and step willingly
into the cattle cars

of our routines
and race toward
the gas chambers
of life-as-usual,
we'll see this man
on the roadside,
and others just like him,
madmen, prophets,
preaching rebellion,
revolution, insurrection, now!
They roar up to the heavens!
They stomp upon the earth!
They wave their hands
as we plod past
and call them
crazy fools!

But you will remember him
as you stand in line.
You will recall his face
as you walk to the edge

of the mass grave
of humanity.
His words will haunt you
as the drumroll starts
as the trigger's pulled
as your body falls
and lies forgotten
with all the others,
as your clothes,
your hair,
your blood,
your eyes,
your lips,
your life
rots down to the bones.
Our truthful bones
stripped bare and stark and white,
undistinguishable from your neighbor's,
jumbled with your enemy's,
robbed of all that separates us now
- race, class, gender,

religion, politics, language -
death, that thief, steals all that,
and leaves only our truthful bones.
Our bones that do not lie
that feel it deep within their marrow
that the madman shouting
on the side of the road
could save us all
if only we would listen.

"Listen," he says,
"you know it in your bones.
The time to change has come.
It's here!
Don't take another step!
Leap to the side!
Bolt from the line!
Race toward this madman
on the side of the road
and run!

Run for your life,
run for our future,
run toward rebellion
from destruction.
It is worth it to run.
It is worth it to struggle.
It is worth all effort to break free!
It is worth risking everything
- and a whole lot more -
to have the tiniest chance to survive!

"But they walk by," he sighs.
"They always walk by,
leaving the madman standing
on the side of the road.

"Listen!
That storm that's coming?
You know what that is?
That's the change stirred up by the
rebels!

It could break you free.
It could save you all from death!
But it won't get here in time
unless you join us!

"Dust we are
and dust we become
and dust ever rises in our footsteps,
but your plodding steps,
your trudging, tired, passive steps,
stir only the sort of grit
that weighs you down,
the grit that stings the eyes,
brings the tears,
clogs your nostrils,
chokes your throat.
The grit that gets kicked
onto those that come behind you.
Until the child
following in your footsteps
gasps.

He scuffs his tired feet,
and the next generation
cannot see,
and so on, and so forth,
until finally,
the last child falls,
crumbles to the ground,
and lies still
until the grit
settles down.
That child will never rise.
What then?
Nothing.
Only the emptiness of failure
of the plodding, passive people
who did not dare to break the line
or the vicious cycle of humanity
through all time.

"Listen to this madman
daring you to run,

to pick up your heels
with courage,
to kick the dust into the sky
to throw your life into rebellion
and churn the storming, coming
winds of change!
I am one,
but we are many,
and your fate is not that pit!
It is not written in the sky
that you will die like cattle
buried in mass graves.

"God's angels do not carry guns.
Soldiers' orders are not divine.

"You were not made out of dust
simply to walk into the grave!
You were made to live!
To sing,
to shout,

to dance,
to struggle for the future,
the children, the earth!
And when Judgment Day arrives,
you will be judged on that!
Did you stand up for all creation,
the saints and sinners, both?
Did you care for the fragile planet
set in motion in the heavens?
Did you follow the age-old teachings
to feed the hungry, heal the sick?
Did you dare to break the line,
that throws children into graves?
Did you listen to this prophet
and join the rebels?

"Hmm?
You, woman!
I'm asking you.
Your heart beats warm
inside your chest,

that loyal dog, your faithful heart,
protector of your home and hearth,
that dog-star heart would die
before it let humanity
go marching off a cliff.
Think on it.
Think carefully on it.
The rebels will be waiting
when you're ready."

Then the madman steps back
and my thoughts shuffle forward
and a veil of dust obscures
the look
burning
in his eyes.

Part Five:
Rebel Song

I was not born to be a rebel.
Few of us are.
I liked my mother's milk,
her smile, her praise, her approval.
My father's voice, I adored.
I cringed when it turned sharp.
I tried to please,
to do my chores,
to sit nicely at the table,
to mind my manners,
study hard,
get good grades,
date nice boys,
to follow my dream,
but come home for Christmas,
to get a job,
support myself,

to not ruin a pleasant evening
with politics or news,
to not argue with my elders,
respect our differences,
or simply don't discuss them . . .

In other words,
in the twenty-first century,
a woman is entitled to her opinion,
as long as she keeps it to herself.
A man can do as he pleases,
so long as he doesn't discuss it
at the dinner table.
And everything is fine,
just so long as we pretend . . .
that the economy is not collapsing,
democracy is not failing,
the ecosystem isn't dying,
first world children are not starving,
the military isn't killing
thousands around the globe,

our school systems are not overcrowded,
our police are not shooting
people for no reason,
our justice system is really just,
our healthcare system actually heals,
our standard diet is nutritional,
and the United States of America
is the greatest nation on Earth!

There is a white noise
that fills the ears.
There is a tremor
shaking in the bones.
Your jaw is locked
from trying to smile
and keep the scream
from coming out.
But your heart feels the truth.
Your bones know the truth.
Your breath breathes the truth
that the madmen speak.

It's not okay.
It's not going to be okay.
It won't ever be okay
if we keep going in this way.

I was not born to be a rebel.
I was not born to have to struggle.
I was not born to have to fight
for my life.

But the lines in the sand
have been drawn across my doorstep,
and my mother's door,
my father's door,
my neighbor's, brother's, sister's door,
and we are marching in a line toward
the pit of our extinction
as democracy falls
in shards of shrapnel
all around.

The madman on the road
is calling to my soul,
but the brand of the rebel
marks for life.
Rebel is an 'R'
seared into your chest.
It burns your flesh,
aches your heart,
it's where the soldiers take their aim.
The mantle of the rebel
sits heavy on the shoulders.
I was not born to be a rebel.
I don't like to break the rules.
I like to stop completely
at the stop signs,
drive the speed limit, exactly,
fill out forms correctly.
I like the pat on the head,
the gold star of approval,
the dog treat for good behavior.
I would prefer to wag my tail

as they sing the national anthem.
I would curl up at my master's feet,
come to his command,
wait expectantly by the door,
patiently endure the chain
around my neck,
eat the scraps from the table,
guard the master's house
like a good soldier of the nation,
protect his children,
bark at strangers,
growl at his enemies,
snap at all who trespass,
attack when he says, sic 'em!
Grab the opposition by the throat!
Rip their flesh apart!
Grrwwww, grrrawwr, grrraowl!

But, I am not a dog.
Even my heart is not that kind of dog.
I am a human being,

a person, a woman,
and when they treat me like a bitch,
and kick me in the ribs,
when they work me like a dog,
and shun me like a mongrel . . .

Then I will turn away
from the hand that feeds me,
the hand that whips me,
beats me, abuses me,
the hand that steals my children,
drowns them, sells them,
the hand that locks up
my fellow women,
neuters them, fixes them,
the hand that feeds us poisoned food,
and leaves us to moan in agony,
the hand that keeps us
working at the spit,
turning roasting, dripping meat
for our wealthy master's feast

while our ribs protrude
and our eyes roll white
and rest becomes a dream we chase
like an elusive rabbit
through the waking nightmare
of our lives until the alarm clock shrills
and jolts us back to work.
If I am a dog, I'm at the end of my rope,
padding in exhaustion
down the dusty road towards death,
trying to stop, to sleep, to rest,
yanked by the hand
of the master.

"Wake up," says the madman.
"Break free," he urges,
calling to me gently
in a far-off coyote's cry.

"Wake up!" snaps the madman,
with a clap of his hands,

as his coyote howl tone
turns mocking.

"Go ahead, then dog.
Farewell," he says,
"March to your death
by the hand of your master.
He will not cry when he kills you.
But I will mourn,
a madman, singing
your funeral dirge
at the dusty edge
of your grave.
Even now I mourn.
I lament your living death,
how your pride has fallen,
your beauty faded,
your spirit lost,
you dog,
you mongrel,
you curr."

"Stop that!" I snap.

"Oh! So you're alive then, dog?"
he retorts.

"Don't call me dog," I snarl.

"Dog," he mocks, "you'd break free
if you were a woman.
I dare you.
I double dare you.
I dee double dare you.
I double DOG dare you . . ."

"That's it!" I snap!
I strain! I stretch.
Rise!
Run!
Leap to the side!
Bolt from the line!
Race with the madman

on the side of the road,
and run!

I run as they shoot.
I run as they chase.
I run as the others watch in fear.

I follow in the footsteps
of the rebel on the road.
With lungs burning fire,
I run!

I run towards life.
Run for the future.
Run in rebellion from destruction!
It is worth it to run.
It is worth it to struggle.
It is worth all effort to break loose.
It is worth risking everything
- and a whole lot more -
to have the tiniest chance . . . to be free!

Now I am the madwoman
on the side of the road,
branded by the 'R' of the rebel.
Run, rebel, run,
see the rebel run,
listen to the coyote-call I howl!
I dance to the heavens.
I stomp upon the earth.
When the moon rises,
the sun sets,
and the planet turns around,
I lift my rebel song to the sky!

If you love life, live!
If you have hope, rise!
If you are a human
- not a dog -
snap the leash!
The master's hand may feed you,
but the food is laced with poison
and you must grovel

to get a place by his fire.
You guard his babies
while your own children suffer,
and for scraps he will work you
to the bone.

Oh, those bones,
those truthful bones
that know that death lies ahead.
Feel those bones,
how the heel-bones dig,
how the breast-bone yearns,
how the ear-bones turn
to hear this rebel woman's song.

Life as usual is a march toward death.
Don't take another step.
Leap to the side.
Bolt from the line.
Race towards the rebels
on the side of the road.

We make no promises.
Our way is dangerous.
Our lives uncertain.
No roof but the stars.
No bed but the ground.
No home but this Earth.
No friend but Truth.
This is the song of the rebel . . .

When the world says die,
the rebel lives!
When the powerful say, kneel,
the rebel stands!
When society says, go,
the rebel comes close.
When they dictate despair,
the rebel hopes.
When they outlaw life,
the rebel thrives.
And when they mandate hate,
the rebel loves.

The rebel is a mother
with a child inside her.
The rebel is a daughter
falling in love.
The rebel is a man
with his head held high.
The rebel is you.
The rebel is I.
We carry in our hearts,
the light of the future.
The torch of life
burns in us.
You can see in our eyes,
the glow of the spirit,
and as all falls
into darkness,
we still shine!

So run to the light.
Run to life.
Run to the ranks of the rebels.

If you love life, live!
If you have hope, rise!
If you're ready, come . . .

Be a rebel.

Author's Note
by
Rivera Sun

Rebel Song is a long poem, woven with metaphor and laced with meaning. In the interest of clarity - and to spare future literature students the agony of guesswork - allow me to share my intentions behind certain themes witha few key points. One, in particular, deserves excruciating specificity: the actions of the rebels.

The rebel archetype is often framed in our collective psyche by violence and opposition. In Rebel Song, and in much of my life's work, I rebel against the confines of that framing. The modern rebel rejects violence as an outdated weapon of oppressors, and instead, embraces active nonviolence as a liberating tool of empowerment.

I felt compelled to articulate this in an author's note because poetry and metaphor are not taught in our schools with the same frequency as the myth of violence. We see violence portrayed as the miracle answer to our problems in nearly every movie, book, television series, foreign policy, or response to social unrest or economic challenge. Because of this cultural overemphasis, it is possible for readers to miss this understated aspect of the weaving metaphors of Rebel Song, and to imagine the rebels armed by the same old, same old tactics of violence.

As my friend Michael Nagler once said, "The problem with violence is that it's just not radical enough for me." After millenniums of extreme violence, there's hardly anything rebellious about it. It's commonplace and generally used as a weapon of oppressive force. According to recent research, it is also less effective than its alternative: organized nonviolent struggle.

The art of turning individual rebellion into mass collective action is called nonviolent struggle. Rebel Song does not have a chapter detailing all the methods and strategies of this field. This work has been covered by a number of other writers, including Gene Sharp in *Waging Nonviolent Struggle*, War Resisters' International in *The Handbook for Nonviolent Campaigns*, and many others, including my own *Dandelion Insurrection Study Guide to Making Change Through Nonviolent Action*. Gaining this knowledge is, in my opinion, one of the most essential tasks for any modern rebel. Not only are the tools of nonviolent action useful in addressing the many crises we face today, but they are also the tools of maintaining a functional democratic society that values liberty, responsibility, sustainability, equality, and justice.

The knowledge of nonviolent struggle comes to us through the hard won efforts of millions upon millions of our fellow human beings who have marched, blockaded, boycotted, gone on strike, built new systems, organized, picketed, engaged in civil disobedience, non-cooperated, shut-down, sat-in, and so much more. These tools of nonviolent action have been used in every nation on Earth for nearly every social justice cause imaginable. Quite simply, there is no tyranny strong enough to withstand the organized determination of ordinary people who refuse to cooperate with injustice.

In Rebel Song, the key to understanding why the rebels are nonviolent lies in examining the complex metaphor of the Storm. As another powerful archetype, the Storm looms large in our human psyche as a powerful and dangerous force. It is important to me that my readers understand the manner in which it has been invoked, and how that informs the perspective on the rebels.

First, the Storm appears as a looming unknown approaching in the night. The narrator sends her dog-heart out to investigate - a metaphor for tapping into inner wisdom and intuitive sensing.

Second, soldiers arrive at the door. They are not the Storm. They are opportunists, riding the edge of the Storm.

Third, the dog-heart reports back, repeating what the Storm says on its own behalf. "I am change and nothing more," the Storm explains, delivering a warning about the nature of change at a time of great injustice. If you stack a tower of injustice high enough, it will inevitably topple and fall.

Fourth, the Madman, also known as the Rebel says, "You see that Storm? It is the dust stirred up by the rebels." Here is where it is important to be clear: The Madman does not (for several reasons) say: the Storm is the rebels, or that the rebels will upend the Big House and the partiers. No, the actions of the rebels stir up the dust of the Storm, which is change and nothing more. So, what, exactly, are these actions taken by the rebels? For that we can look further in the Rebel Song . . .

where it says the rebels live. Love. Stand. Come closer. Hope. Thrive. Rise. Dance. Sing. Turn toward life. Break free of chains. These are the actions by which the rebels stir up the dust of change and set in motion the Storm that unravels systems of injustice, levels inequality, and ends oppression. The rebels resist injustice by love, life, hope - not by "any means necessary".

If we look around our society, we can see how oppressive forces try to keep our love chained to platitudes and holiday cards, preventing love from breaking free to sing in the streets or treat all human beings with dignity and respect. Life is tied to the turning spit that roasts meat for some, while others go hungry. But it is not by violence that we free love and life from these chains. No, as Étienne de La Boétie said, "I do not ask that you place hands upon the tyrant to topple him over, but simply that you support him no longer; then you will behold him, like a great Colossus whose pedestal has been pulled away, fall of his own weight and break in pieces."

So, it is with this strategic understanding in mind that I make the clear and unequivocal declaration that the rebels in this poem, and indeed, many of the true rebels in our contemporary world, are those who practice active, organized nonviolent struggle. Furthermore, the modern rebel must also break past the limitations of a solely oppositional stance. Today's rebels must expand their vision beyond the box of what they are rebelling against. We must stand for our principles and visions. We must turn toward life, run toward love, and rebel in the direction of dignity, respect, justice, equality, nonviolence, peace, care of the Earth, and hope.

This is what I believe in.
This is how I move into action.
This is my Rebel Song.

Rivera Sun

About the Author

Rivera Sun is the author of *Billionaire Buddha, The Dandelion Insurrection, The Way Between* and other novels, as well as nine plays, a study guide to nonviolent action, a book of poetry, and numerous articles. She has red hair, a twin sister, and a fondness for esoteric mystics. She went to Bennington College to study writing as a Harcourt Scholar and graduated with a degree in dance. She lives in an earthship house in New Mexico, where she grows tomatoes, bakes sourdough bread, and writes poetry, plays, and novels on the side. Rivera has been an aerial dancer, a bike messenger, and a gung-fu style tea server. Everything else about her - except her writing - is perfectly ordinary.

**Other Works
by
Rivera Sun**

Rebel Song, Audio Version
The Dandelion Insurrection
The Roots of Resistance
Billionaire Buddha
The Way Between
Steam Drills, Treadmills, and Shooting Stars
The Dandelion Insurrection Study Guide
to Strategic Nonviolent Action
Skylandia: Farm Poetry From Maine
Freedom Stories: Volume One
The Imagine-a-nation of Lala Child

Connect with Rivera!

Email: rivera@riverasun.com
Facebook: Rivera Sun
Twitter: @RiveraSunAuthor
Website: www.riverasun.com

If you liked Rebel Song, you'll love
The Dandelion Insurrection

A rare gem of a book, a must read, it charts the way
forward in this time of turmoil and transformation." -
Velcrow Ripper, director Occupy Love,
Genie Award Winner

"When fear is used to control us, love is how we rebel!"

Under a gathering storm of tyranny, Zadie Byrd Gray whirls into the life of Charlie Rider and asks him to become the voice of the Dandelion Insurrection. With the rallying cry of life, liberty, and love, Zadie and Charlie fly across America leaving a wake of revolution in their path. Passion erupts. Danger abounds. The lives of millions hang by a thin thread of courage, but in the midst of the madness, the golden soul of humanity blossoms . . . and miracles start to unfold!

"THE handbook for the coming revolution!"
- Lo Daniels, Editor of Dandelion Salad

"This novel will not only make you want to change the world, it will remind you that you can." - Gayle Brandeis, author of *The Book of Dead Birds*, winner of the Bellwether Prize for Socially Engaged Fiction

"Close your eyes and imagine the force of the people and the power of love overcoming the force of greed and the love of power. Then read *The Dandelion Insurrection*. In a world where despair has deep roots, *The Dandelion Insurrection* bursts forth with joyful abandon."
- Medea Benjamin, Co-founder of CodePink

"*The Dandelion Insurrection* is an updated, more accurate, less fantastical *Brave New World* or *1984*."
- David Swanson, author, peace and democracy activist

". . . a beautifully written book just like the dandelion plant itself, punching holes through the concept of corporate terror and inviting all to join in the insurrection."
- Keith McHenry,
Co-founder of the Food Not Bombs Movement

"A fundamentally political book with vivid characters and heart stopping action. It's a must and a great read."
- Judy Rebick, activist and author of *Occupy This!*

Now Available! *The Roots of Resistance*,
sequel to *The Dandelion Insurrection!*

Charlie Rider and Zadie Byrd Gray may have won a
revolution, but "they've got more problems than centipedes
have legs" – as lawyer Tansy Beaulisle

puts it. The new president can't be
trusted. The rich and powerful refuse
to step down. A mysterious group
called the Roots slips a violent edge
into the heart of the movement.
When the media cooks up a love
affair between Zadie and the Roots'
leader, it takes every ounce of
Charlie's courage and compassion to
keep the Dandelion Insurrection
moving forward.

*"The Roots of Resistance offers an inspiring story to help guide
love-based strategic change."*
- Tom Atlee, Co-Intelligence Institute

*"If you loved Starhawk's "Fifth Sacred Thing"… you will drink
in this must-read page-turner!"* - Rosa Zubizarreta

Printed in Poland
by Amazon Fulfillment
Poland Sp. z o.o., Wrocław

50971861R00060